합기도를 응용한 글로벌 호신술!

Global self-defense with Hapkido!

생활 안전 호신술

Self-defense Survival Techniques

저자 이기세·DAMIAN·노성환·최영진·천인순·김현동

Author Lee, Ki-Se · DAMIAN ADAMS · No, Sung-Hwan · Choi, Young-Jin · Cheon, In-Soon · Kim, Hyun-Dong

도서출판 진영사

생활 안전 호신술

이기세 · DAMIAN · 노성환 · 최영진 · 천인순 · 김현동

2019년 05월 22일 초판 인쇄
2019년 05월 28일 초판 발행

발행인 박 진 영
발행처 도서출판 진영사
인천광역시 부평구 갈산동 185번지 풍진빌딩 303호
전화 : 032)505-4207
팩스 : 032)505-4206
E-mail : 0183734207@hanmail.net
등록 : 122-91-77317

ISBN 978-89-6541-438-4 93350
정가 15,000원

목 차
(Mokcha-Contents)

머 리 말
(Meolimal-Preface)

최근 문재인 정부에서는 국민들의 안전한 사회를 지향할 목적으로 자치경찰제를 2019년에 5개 광역시도에서 실시한다고 발표하였으며, 2021년도까지 전국에 확대 실시한다고 발표하였다.

사회 안전과 관련하여 최근에 빈번히 발생하고 있는 묻지마 폭행, 데이트폭력, 학교폭력 사건들이 증가하고 있는 가운데 자신을 보호할 수 있는 호신술이나 다양한 무도의 수련은 반드시 필요한 시기라고 강조해도 과하지 않다.

본 교재는 두려운 일상생활에서 벗어나고자 하는 많은 국민들의 입장에서 생각하여 남녀노소 누구나 쉽게 익혀서 활용할 수 있는 쉬운 호신술을 사진과 설명으로 쉽게 이해하고 실전에서 사용 가능할 수 있도록 편집을 하였다. 또한 글로벌 무도를 지향하는 국내의 무도지도자들과 동양무도에 관심이 있으며 특히 한국무술에 남다른 애착을 가지고 있는 호주과학자출신 Damian Adams와 함께 한국의 전통무술인 합기도를 응용하여 자기방어를 할 수 있도록 글로벌 생활안전 호신술 교본을 엮었으며, 많은 사람들이 관심을 갖고 책에 나와 있는 호신술만이라도 단한번씩만 연습을 한다면 충분한 효과가 있을 것으로 기대를 한다.

저자일동

Preface

Recently, Moon Jae-in, the South Korean President announced that the government will introduce a self-policing system in five metropolitan cities in 2019. The aim is to promote a safe society of the people. This initiative will expand nationwide by 2021. It is important to emphasize that self-defense and various martial arts training can help someone protect themselves in times of increasing violent incidents in general society, schools etc. This textbook was edited to help both men and women, young or old, to understand some easy self-defense techniques that can be readily mastered and implemented with practice by following the photos and descriptions.

I have brought together domestic Korean Martial Arts leaders and Damian Adams, an Australian scientist and Korean Martial Arts instructor to create a global martial arts textbook for self-defense by applying Hapkido, a traditional Korean Martial Art. To truly master martial arts takes a life-time of study and practice, however, it is hoped that the simple techniques presented in this book will assist the reader in protecting themselves with minimal practice.

All author

제 1 장 단전강화법

>>> (Danjeon kanghwa beop - Abdominal strengthening method)

단전강화법은 인체의 중앙부라고 할 수 있는 배꼽(제대부)아래쪽에 있는 기해(氣海)라는 혈자리 주변을 강화하여 인체의 순환기능을 강화하는데 있어 도움이 될 수 있도록 호흡법을 이용하여 인체를 강화하는 방식중의 하나이다. 일명 "단전 호흡법"이라고도 하며, 방식으로는 기합과 동작을 통해 반복적으로 장기간 지속함으로서 근육의 강도 및 기합소리의 크기와 자신감이 향상되도록 하는 정적인 운동법의 하나이다.

Abdominal (Danjeon) breathing is one of the methods of strengthening the human body. The Danjeon is located below the navel (umbilicus) and is often stated to be the source of energy as well as a person's center of gravity. Danjeon breathing involves using the abdomen rather than just the chest to bring air into the lungs. These excercises not only strengthen the abdomen but also the entire core which also includes such areas as the meridian Gihae (BL 24), known as the Sea of Energy which reportedly assists circulation. Danjeon kanghwa beop is a group of static exercises which through repeated practice will improve muscle strength and self-confidence.

1) **단전호흡(5수)**: 단전호흡은 기해(氣海)라고 하는 혈자리 주변을 강화하기 위하여 들숨과 날숨을 조절하여 인체의 기(氣)흐름을 원활하게하기 위하여 실시하는 호흡을 통한 운동 방법이다. 동작에 따라 기합소리와 구령을 병행하여 실시하는 것을 원칙으로 한다.

The five Danjeon breathing exercises are used to control inhalation and exhalation in order to strengthen the surrounding area of the meridian Gihae. In principle, the movement is performed simultaneously with the shout (kihap) and is dependent on the exercise being performed. There will typically be a period of holding the breath between inhalation and exhalation in which the abdomen is tensed.

구분	사진	방 법
기짜기 준비자세		〈 기짜기 기본자세는 도복의 허리띠를 잡고 다리를 붙이고 정면을 보고 선다. To start hold your belt while standing upright facing the front with your feet together.

기짜기

준비자세

머리와 허리를 숙여 인사를 한다. ▷
Bow at the waist with your head down.

◁ 두 손을 단전 앞에서 모아 서로 교차시킨 후
Cross your hands in front of your Danjeon (keep your hands flat)

기짜기

준비자세

정면 앞에서
다시 교차 시킨 후 ▷
Complete the circle and bring your hands up from in front of your Danjeon to infront of your chest with your hands crossed

◁ 등주먹이 아래로 향하게 한 후 양쪽 허리 옆에 댄다.
Bring both hands to your waist while creating a fist. The backs of your hands should be down with your palms up.

기짜기 준비자세

단전호흡의 차렷 자세에서
양쪽 앞꿈치를
45도 벌리고 ▷
While in this attention stance of Danjeon breathing, turn the front of your feet out at 45 degrees

◁ 다음은 발 뒷꿈치를
45도 벌린다.
Next, open your heels out 45 degrees.

기짜기 준비자세

다시 양쪽 발 앞꿈치를
45도 벌리고 ▷
Repeat the above foot motion again by turning the front of the feet out at 45 degree

◁ 다시 발뒷꿈치를 45도
벌리면서 기마자세로
자세를 낮춘다.
Repeat the heals out then front of feet out one more time each until your legs are wide apart as shown in the picture. Bend your knees to sit down in what is commonly known as a horse-riding stance.

기짜기

1수

◁ 양손이 허리에서 앞으로 나가면서 크게 기합소리를 낸다.

Open your hands with fingers wide apart, and as you start to push them forward, yell abruptly.

양손을 앞쪽으로 뻗으면서 손가락을 펴며 숨을 코로들여 마신다. ▷

With both hands stretched forward, raise your arms slowly, and breathe in slowly through your nose.

기
짜
기

1수

◁ 무릎과 양손이 펴지면서 마지막 까지 숨을 들여 마시는데 이때 총 여덟을 세는 동안 동작이 이루어지도록 한다.

Gradualy raise your arms and at the same time slowly straighten your knees during a count of 8 while continuing to breathe in deeply.

무릎과 양손이 여덟 번째에 모두 편다. ▷

When you reach the count of 8 your knees should be straight and your arms up high as in the picture.

기짜기 1수

위로 뻗었던 손을 뒤쪽으로 내린 후 ▷

Bend your arms at the elbows and slowly bring your hands down next to your head while holding your breath and tensing your abdomen

◁ 다시 양손이 앞으로 뻗어 나오면서 입으로 공기를 불어 낸다.

Stretch both hands out forward of your body and breathe out slowly through your mouth.

바깥쪽으로 양손을 펼치면서 마무리 한다. ▷

Circle both arms horizontally outwards to finish the first exercise.

기
짜
기

2수

◁ 양손이 허리에서 어깨 쪽으로 올라온다.

For the second exercise bring both hands down towards the Danjeon and in preparation to raise them up to shoulder level.

이때 크게 기합을 내면서 손바닥이 지면을 향하도록 한 후 아래로 밀어 내린다.

▷

When you get to shoulder level turn your hands so that they are palm down then kihap.

기
짜
기

2수

◁ 양손이 단전 주변까지 내려오면 양손바닥이 위쪽을 향하도록 한다.
When both hands reach the vicinity of Danjeon, turn both hands so that the palms are facing upwards.

다시 양손바닥이 위쪽을 향하도록 하여 끌어 올린다. ▷
Gradually bring both hands back up.

기
짜
기

2수

이때 무릎을 펴고 마지막
숨을 들여 마시면서 ▷
At this point, straighten
your knees and finish
breathing in.

◁ 양손이 얼굴까지
올라오면서 공기를 입으로
불어내기 시작한다.
Bring both hands up in
front of your face, turn
them back to palm down,
and start to stretch them
out in front while gradually
exhale out of your mouth.

마지막 동작으로
손을 바깥쪽으로 펴서
가슴을 확장 시키는 동작을
한다. ▷
Continue to circle your
arms out horizontally till
they are out to the side to
finish the second exercise.

기짜기

3수

〈 기마자세에서 양손을 어깨 넓이로 앞으로 뻗어 편다.

While dropping back down to a horse-rising stance extend both arms directly in front of your body shoulder width apart and breathe in through the nose.

엄지와 검지를 뺀 나머지 손가락을 안쪽으로 약간 휘게 한 후 〉

Bend your arms back toward your body and bend your wrists so that your fingers and thumbs point back towards your body

기짜기

3수

《 팔을 접어 양손을 목 앞쪽까지 끌어당긴 후
Bend your arms and bring your hands up in front of your neck

순간적으로 빠르게 양손을 뻗는다. 이런 동작을 연속하여 세 번을 반복하도록 하며 이때 숨을 멈춘 후 동작을 반복하도록 한다. 》
Extend both arms and hands out rapidly and kihap. Repeat this action three times in a row. At this point, stop breathing and repeat the action.

기
짜
기

◁ 양손을 뻗어 어깨선과 나란히 한 후

Circle the arms vertically until both arms are stretched out at shoulder level while breathing out through the mouth to finish the third excercise

4수

기합소리와 함께 양손을 가슴 쪽 앞에서 교차 시킨다. ▷

To start the fourth exercise, cross your hands in front of your chest with your hands clenched into fists and kihap.

기 짜 기

4수

◁ 다시 교차된 양손을 무릎 바깥쪽으로 펼치며 재기합을 낸 후, 바위를 들어 올리듯이 천천히 무릎을 편다.

Open both hands and drop them quickly to outside the line of the knee, slowly straighten your knees and raise your arms as if you are lifting a rock. Do this for a count of 8 while breathing in slowly through your nose.

무릎이 펴지면서 양손이 머리 쪽에 도달하면 ▷

You should end up with your knees straight and your arms at head level

기짜기

4수

◁ 팔은 머리 뒤쪽으로 뿌리치며

Circle your arms backward to bring your hands back behind your head

양손을 앞으로 뻗으면서 입으로 공기를 불어낸다. ▷

Then extend both arms forward hands as you start to exhale slowly through your mouth.

◁ 마지막으로 양손을 바깥쪽으로 펼치면서 마무리 한다.

Continue to circle your arms horizontally till your arms are to your side at shoulder level to finish the fourth exercise.

기짜기

5수

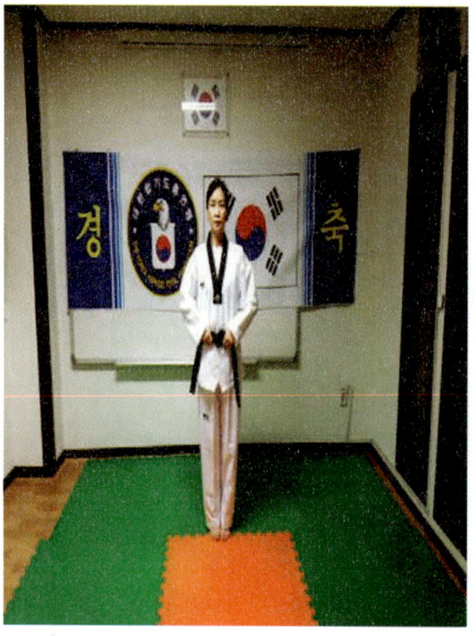

〈 바르게 선 자세에서

To start the fifth exercise come back to an attention stance while holding your belt, feet together and looking forward

기합소리와 함께 오른쪽방향으로 무릎을 굽히면서 양손을 동시에 뻗어 올린다. 〉

Step to the right into a front bending stance in which your front leg is bent but your rear leg is straight. Kihap as you stretch your hands downward and forward.

기 짜 기

5수

◁ 이때 코로 공기를 들여 마시면서 동작을 지속하며 눈은 양 손끝을 보도록 한다.

Breathe in slowly through your nose while keeping your eyes on the tips of your hands as you gradually raise them up

양손과 뒤쪽 다리가 사선형태를 이루면 동작을 멈춘 후 ▷

When both hands and rear legs are aligned, the movement is completed. This should take a count of 8 to get to this position

◁ 몸은 정면을 주시하며 양손을 허리 쪽으로 내리며 마무리 한다.

Bring your right foot back to an attention stance and continue to raise your arms until they are straight up. The body looks forward and ends with both hands down toward the waist.

기짜기

5수

◁ 바르게 선 자세에서

Then continue to circle your hands back to your head while bending your elbows as you have done previously, then extend your arms in front of your body while breathing out through your mouth slowly

다시 왼쪽 방향으로 무릎을 굽히며 양손을 모아 ▷

Repeat the movement you have just completed to the right side, this time to the left. Step to the left into a front bending stance in which your front leg is bent but your rear leg is straight. Kihap as you stretch your hands downward and forward

기
짜
기

5수
(좌)

◁ 허리쪽에서 위쪽으로 양손을 뻗으면서 코로 숨을 들여 마신다. 여덟 동작까지 지속 한 후

Breathe in slowly through your nose while keeping your eyes on the tips of your hands as you gradually raise them up for a count of 8

몸은 정면을 보면서 양팔을 올린 후 ▷

The body looks forward, raises your hands

◁ 양손을 앞으로 뻗으면서 입으로는 공기를 불어내면서 마무리 한다.

Come back to an attention stance with your arms vertical while looking to the front.

제 2 장 >>> 전환도법

(Jeonhwan do beop-Stepping method)

전환도법은 자신의 몸을 가볍게 움직이는 회전법의 일종으로 과거에는 보법이라는 용어를 많이 활용하였다. 도법은 무도를 행하면서 필요에 따라 회전을 통해 상대의 공격을 방어하며, 공격 시 회전력을 조절하여 강도를 조절할 수 있는 움직임의 일종이다. 단순도법도 있지만 회전도법이 좀 더 우아하면서도 회전력의 영향으로 강한 힘을 발현시킬 수 있는 장점이 있다.

The stepping method implements rotation of the body as a person is stepping and shifting their body which gives the impression that they are moving lightly. This light stepping movement with rotation has at times been described as giving a martial art its beauty or providing the art component of martial arts. This method of stepping is a means to defend against an attack using rotational force. There are simpler and more direct ways of defending an attack, however, using a rotational force while stepping is a more elegant means of defending oneself. It does not require great physical strength of the defendant in using force on force as some simpler methods employ, but rather allows a defender to redirect the attackers force. Thereby using the attackers force against themselves through the use of rotation. Jeonhwan do beop or Jeonhwan beop for short literally translates as conversion method. It can be thought of as converting rotationl force created through stepping into a defence against the attacker's force which then converts into your own attack.

1) 일반 전환법(General stepping method)

전환법은 공격과 방어를 원활히 하기 위한 고급 보법으로 회전 속도에 따라 술기의 강도를 조절할 수 있다.

The stepping (conversion) method is an advanced method to facilitate borth defence and attack. The strength of the skill can be controlled according to the speed of rotation.

전
환
법

1수

전환법 1수(Stepping method number 1)

◁ 전환법 1수는 왼발을 앞에 놓고 손의 위치는 허리 쪽에 둔다.

Start with your left foot forward in a back-bending stance, your left-hand palm down in front of your waist and your right hand behind your back.

뒤쪽에 있는 오른발이 앞으로 나오면서 허리에 있던 팔을 편다. ▷

As you start to step your right foot forward start unfolding your arms.

전환법

1수

◁ 양팔의 위치를 바꾸면서 회전을 실시한다.
Continue the forward motion and rotation while repositioning both arms.

처음 섰던 위치에서 방향을 180도로 바꾸어 선다. ▷
Complete the stepping and roatating motion by then bringing the left foot forward and turning your body a full 180 degrees. You will now be in a mirror image posture to that which you started.

전환법 2수

전환법 2수(Stepping method number 2)

◁ 전환법 2수는 왼발을 앞에 놓고 손의 위치는 허리 쪽에 둔다.

Start with your left foot forward in a back-bending stance, your left-hand palm down in front of your waist and your right hand behind your back. You are starting the same as method number 2.

뒤쪽에 있는 오른발이 앞으로 1보 나온 후 ▷

Start to step your right foot forward while unfolding your arms across your waist

전환법

2수

◁ 맨 처음 시작 때의 자세로 동작을 바꾼 후
Complete the step forward such that your arms and body position will be opposite to the starting position (opposite side forward), except standard up straight

180도 회전을 하여 선다.▷
The step your left foot forward followed by your right and make a circular step such that you will make a full 180 degree turn. You will now be in the same posture with same side forward as you started.
Note: Stepping method number 2 is the same as number 1 except there is a single step forwards before the 180-degree rotation steps.

전환법

3수

전환법 3수(Stepping method number 3)

◁ 전환법 3수는 왼발을 앞에 놓고 손의 위치는 허리 쪽에 둔다.

Start with your left foot forward in a back-bending stance, your left-hand palm down in front of your waist and your right hand behind your back.

전환법 1수와 동일하게 180도 회진을 한 후 ▷

Start performing the 180 degree rotation steps as described in method number 1

전환법

3수

◁ 1번과 같이 자세를 잡은 후

You will now be at the finish of stepping method number 1

오른발을 1보 뒤쪽으로 이동시키며 자세를 잡는다.

▷

Now finish by stepping your right foot backwards and changing your hand positions.

Note: Stepping method number 3 is the same as number 1 except there is a single step backwards after the 180-degree rotation steps.

2) 4방 전환법(Four-way stepping method)

4방 전환법은 +(열십자) 방향으로 움직이면서 공격과 방어를 하기 위한 자세를 갖추는 동작으로 속도는 매우 빠르게 움직여야 한다.

The four-way stepping method should move smoothly and fast. It is a means of attacking and defending while moving in the pattern of a cross.

4방 전한법

◁ 전환법의 기본 자세로 선 후

Stand in the basic starting position as described previously

4 방 전환법

전환법 1수와 같이 몸을 전환시켜 180도로 움직여 이동한 후 ▷

Perform the 180-degree steps as described for method number 1

◁ 정면을 기준으로 270도 회전을 한다.

Make a 270-degree turn towards the front, by shifting your left foot then your right.

4 방 전환법

다시 앞쪽으로 180도
회전을 한 후 ▷
Then make a 180-degree
turn forwards

◁ 90도 회전을 하여 맨
처음 선 자리로 이동한다.
Finally, make a 90-degree
turn to finish in the
starting location and
posture.

제3장 기초 자세 잡기

(Gicho jase jabki-Basic stances)

기초 자세 잡기는 무도를 하면서 필요한 기초체력을 향상시키기 위하여 실시하는 정적 트레이닝의 일종이다.

특히 이 자세들을 강화하면 권법이나 다른 무도 동작을 응용하는데 매우 큰 도움이 된다.

Basic stances can be performed as static training to improve physical strength and stamina. Strengthening through the practice of these postures is particularly very helpful for the application of force while performing martial art and self-defence techniques as they provide a solid foundation for the generation of force. Without a good foundation provided by solid stances our techniques will be weak.

동작	설 명
	1) 기마자세 – Gima jase 다리를 어깨보다 약간 넓게 조정한 후 무릎을 굽혀 앉은 후 두 손을 뻗어 자세를 취한다. 사람이 말을 탄 자세와 비슷하다고 하여 기마자세라고 하였다. The feet should be slightly wider than the shoulders, bend your knees such that you are "sitting down" and stretch out your hands as shown in the picture. This stance is often called horse-riding stance.
	2) 사선앉기 - Saseon anjgi 몸의 형상이 사선을 이루듯, 한쪽 무릎을 접고 앉고 다른 다리는 쭉 펴서 양 손이 대각 평형을 이루도록 자세를 취한다. Sitting on the diagonal. Sit with one knee bent while the other leg is stretched out. Most of your weight should be supported by the bent leg. Straighten your arms with open hands such that palms are up and that the arms form a straight diagonal line that follow the line created by your straight leg.

3) 외발서기 - Oebal seogi

다리 한쪽을 들고 중심을 잡는 자세로 다리를 들고 서있는 쪽의 손을 사마귀의 모습으로 한 후 자세를 취한다. (독립식이라고도 한다)

Stand up straight on one leg, with the bent leg positioned such the sole of the foot is touching the inside of the knee of the straight leg. Bend the same sided arm to 90-degrees and position your hand in the shape of the praying mantis, with the other hand held underneath that arm also in praying mantis.

4) 낮은 앉기 - Najeun anjgi

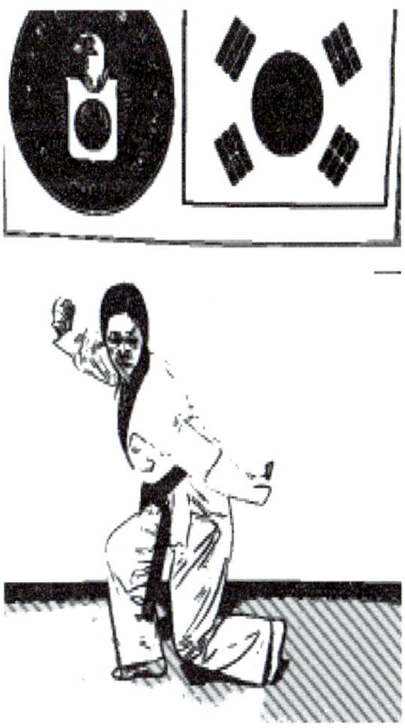

무릎을 90도 구부리고 앉은 후 다른 무릎도 바닥에 가깝도록 낮은 자세를 취한다. 이때 손은 대각으로 수평을 이루게 한 후 손끝을 세워 자세를 취한다. (낮은 산과 비슷하다고 하여 소등산이라고도 한다)

Bend one leg to 90 degrees to sit down low with your other knee almost touching the floor. The front arm should be bent and hold horizontally at head height with your hand in the praying mantis position. Your rear arm should be held diagonally down also with the hand curled back into the praying mantis position. This stance is also called Sodeungsan Mountain because of its appearance which is similar to the low mountains of Sodeungsan.

5) 교차 앉기 - Gyocha anjgi

양팔을 수평으로 뻗어 균형을 잡은 후 다리를 꼬아 중심을 아래쪽으로 두고 앉는다.
Stretch your arms out horizontally with wrists bent and palms facing outwards. Cross one leg behind the other with that foot only being on the ball of the foot, while foot of the leg in front should have the entire foot in contact with the ground. Sit down in this stance.

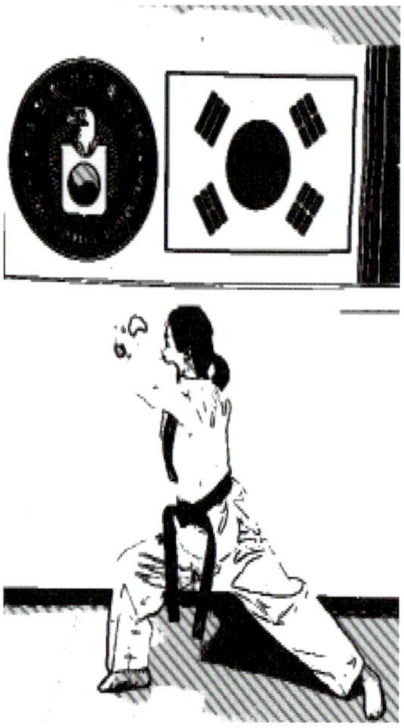

6) 앞서기 - Ap seogi

한쪽 다리를 구부린 후 뒷다리를 뻗어 자세를 취한다. (등산식이라고도 한다)
Bend your front leg such that the lower leg is vertical and stretch the rear leg as shown in the picture. This stance is also called the climbing stance or front bending stance.

7) 공격식 - Gonggyeoksik

상대방과 대련을 할 경우 취하는 자세라 하여 공격자세라고도 한다.
Also called the attack posture or attack stance, it is similar to the horse-rising stance except the feet are truned out 45-degrees and the fists held up in a ready position as shown. This position is often taken when facing an opponent.

8) 헛 다리 서기 - Heos dali seogi

다리의 중심을 뒤에 두고 앞쪽 다리는 가볍게 대고 서있어 어느 쪽에 힘을 주고 있는지를 모르게 서는 자세라 하여 허식이라고도 한다.
Place the front leg in front of the body with very little body weight being held on the ball of the foot while the rear leg is bent slightly and carries the majority of the body weight. Also known as holding the bridge in vain or cat-stance.

제4장 몸풀기 동작

>>> (Mompulki dongjak-Relaxation exercises <warm-up/cool-down>)

몸 풀기는 운동 전에 실시하는 것과 운동 후에 실시하는 것으로 구분을 한다. 몸 풀기의 목적은 운동 상해를 예방하며 동작을 자유스럽게 하는데 도움이 되며 기능을 향상시키는데 큰 역할을 한다. 신체부위별로 팔과 다리, 허리, 몸통 등 신체 전부를 늘리는데 도움이 된다.

Physical relaxation and light stretching excercises should be performed prior to and after practicing martial art or self-defence techniques as a means of warming-up and cooling-down. The purpose of these excercises is to help prevent injury, to free up movement and to improve function. The whole body including the arms, legs, waist, torso etc should be incorporated into these excercises.

동작	설 명
	양손을 깍지 한 후 위쪽으로 뻗어 스트레칭 한다. Link the fingers of both hands together and stretch upwards.
	손바닥을 내보이며 손가락이 지면을 향하게 한 후 스트레칭 한다. With your palm up, use your other hand to pull your fingers down towards the ground.

한손으로 측 머리를 잡고 당기면서 목을 스트레칭 한다.

Stretch your neck by holding and pulling on the side of the head with one hand. Repeat on the other side.

양손을 허리에 대고 상체를 뒤로 늘린다.

Put both hands on the waist and lean the upper body backwards.

한손을 뻗어 다른 손으로 접어서 당기면서 스트레칭을 한다.

Stretch one arm across your body horizontally then use your other arm to hook under it and pull backwards to increase the stretch.

양손을 모아 엄지손가락을 턱에 대고 머리를 들어 위로 스트레칭 한다.

Put your hands together, then place your thumbs under your chin, then lift your head with your hands to stretch your neck upwards.

한손을 머리에 대고 다른 한손으로 팔을 내려
스트레칭 한다.

Place one hand over the top of your head, reaching towards the back. Place the other hand on your bicep to help lower your arm to stretch your neck downwards.

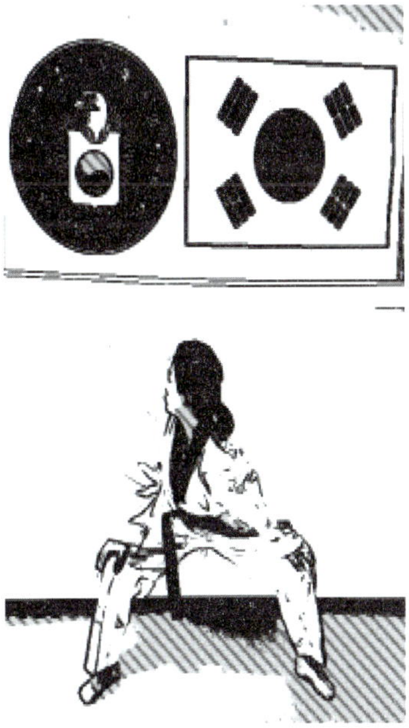

다리를 기마자세로 취한 후 양손을 무릎에 대고
허리를 옆으로 돌려 스트레칭 한다.

Sit down in a horse-riding stance with feet and knees pointed outwards by 45 degrees. Place your hands on your knees then push one shoulder forward while looking over your shoulder to the rear. Repeat on the other side.

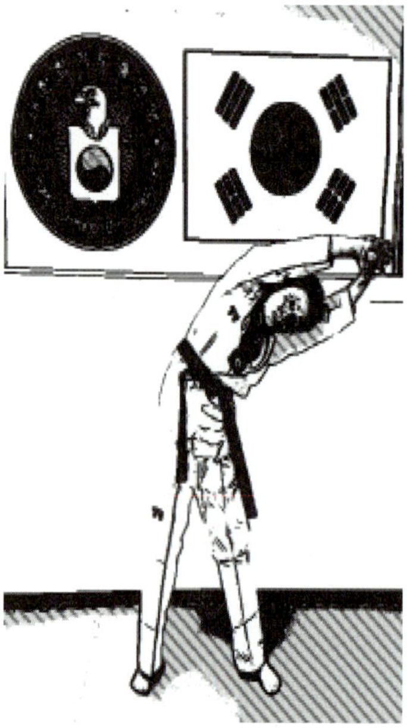

어깨 넓이로 선 후 양손을 잡고 좌우로 스트레칭을 한다.

Stand with your feet shoulder-width apart. Hold both hands together and stretch to the side. Repeat on the other side.

양손을 깍지를 한 후 앞으로 손을 뻗어 스트레칭으로 한나.

Link your fingers together and stretch your hands forward.

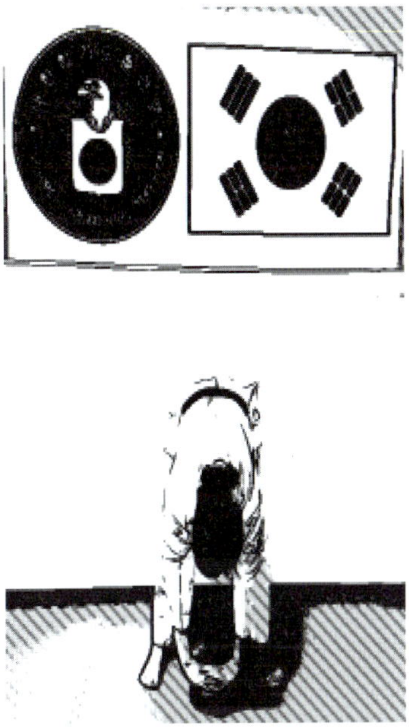

어깨 넓이로 다리를 벌리고 양손을 깍지한 후
허리를 숙이면서 스트레칭을 한다.

Stand with your feet shoulder-width apart. Link your fingers together behind your back and bend forward at the waist.

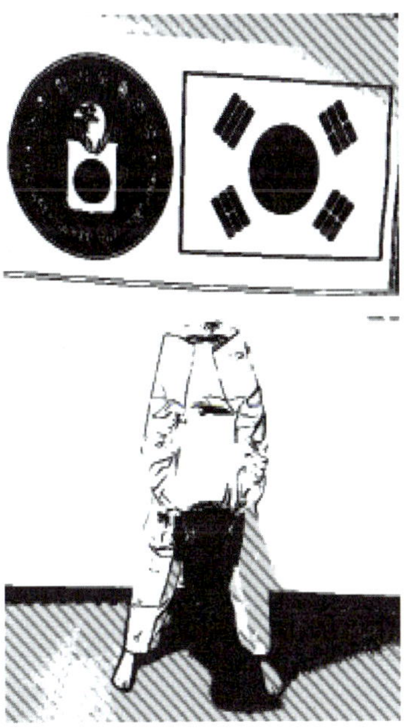

다리를 어깨 넓이로 벌린 후 허리를 숙여
깍지를 한 후 허리를 앞으로 숙여 스트레칭을
한다.

Spread your legs shoulder-wide, then lower your back to make a pod, then stretch your back forward.

벽에 등을 대고 90도 로 앉은 후 한쪽다리를 접어 다른 쪽 무릎위에 놓고 앉는다.

Sit at 90 degrees with your back against the wall. Fold one leg and place it across the other leg as shown. Repeat on the other leg.

벽에 등을 대고 90도 정도로 앉은 후 한쪽 다리를 뻗어 버티는 동작을 실시한다.

Sit at 90 degrees with your back against the wall. Lift on leg straight up to stretch. Repeat n the other leg.

제5장 >>> 기초발차기 (Gicho Balchagi)

기초발차기는 앞차기, 발들어 올리기, 뒷차기, 앉아 돌려차기(앞, 뒤), 옆차기를 사진을 통해 소개하기로 한다.

발차기는 상대방의 공격을 방어하는데 필요하며, 때로는 발을 이용하여 상대방을 공격하는데 쓸 수도 있다. 발등과 발끝, 발날, 뒷꿈치로 다양하게 공격할 수 있다.

Basic kicks will be introduced through photos of front kicks, foot lifts, rear kicks, sit-down kicks and side kicks.

A kick is necessary to defend an opponent's attack, and can sometimes be used to attack an opponent using his feet. You can attack variously with your feet, toes, feet, and heels.

1) 앞차기 (Apchagi-front kick)	앞차기는 상대방을 발로 공격하는 방법이다. A front kick is how you attack your opponent with your feet.

앞서기로 자세를 잡은 후

You're standing in front of him,

무릎을 접어 든 후

After you fold up your knees,

무릎을 펴면서 발끝으로 목표를 공격한다.

Stretch your knee and attack the target with tiptoe.

2) 발올리기 (Balloligi–Raise one foot)	발들어 올리기는 다리를 펴서 얼굴까지 올렸다 내리는 기술이다. The lifting of your feet extended your legs to your face. It's a skill to lower.

앞서기로 자세를 잡은 후

You're standing in front of him,

한쪽 발을 들어 얼굴까지 끌어
올린다.
(다리는 내릴 때 공격한다)

Raise one foot of you to your face.
(Your legs attack your opponent
when you get off.)

3) 돌려차기
(Dollyochagi–Turn kick)

돌려차기는 발등으로 상대방을 공격하는 기술이다.

A kick is a technique to attack an opponent with your feet.

앞서기로 자세를 잡은 후

You're standing in front of him,

무릎을 접은 후

After folding your knees,

무릎을 펴면서 발등으로 상대방을 공격한다.

Stretch your opponent with the back of your feet as you stretch your knees and overpower them.

4) 뒷차기 (Dwichagi-Back kick)	뒷차기는 한쪽발을 축으로 뒤로 돌면서 옆차기로 공격하는 기술이다. Back kick is the technique of attacking an opponent with a side kick, turning one of your feet back to the axis.

앞서기로 자세를 잡은 후
You're standing in front of him,

앞에 있던 발을 고정한 후
시계방향으로 회전 한 후
After fixing the foot in front of you, turn clockwise.

다리를 들어 공격을 한다.
Raise your leg and attack your opponent.

5) 앉아 뒤차기 (Anjadwichagi-Sit-down back kick)	앉아 뒤차기는 상대방의 하단을 공격하고자 할 때 사용하는 기술이다. Sit-down back kick is a technique that you use to lower your posture when you want to attack the opponent's bottom.

앞서기로 자세를 잡은 후
You're standing in front of him,

앞에 있던 다리의 무릎을 지면에 대고
Put your knees in front of you on the ground.

다른 쪽 발로 공격한다.
You attack the other side of your foot.

6) 앉아 앞 돌려차기 (Anjaapdollyochagi–Sit–down forward kick)	앉아 앞 돌려차기는 상대방의 하단을 공격하는 기술로 앞쪽으로 회전하면서 공격하는 기술이다. Sit-down forward kick is a technique where you attack the bottom of an opponent as you rotate forward.

앞서기로 자세를 잡은 후
You're standing in front of him,

앞에 있던 다리를 낮추어 앉은 후
After you lower your leg in front of you,

다리를 뻗어 공격한다.
Stretch your legs forward and attack your opponent.

7) 앉아 뒤 돌려차기 (Anjadwidollyochagi-Sit-and-turn-back)	앉아 뒤돌려차기는 앞다리를 축으로 앉으면서 다른 쪽 다리로 상대방을 공격하는 기술이다. Sit-and-turn-back is the technique of attacking an opponent with your other leg while sitting on your front leg with an axis.

앞서기로 자세를 잡은 후
You're standing in front of him,

앞에 있던 다리를 축으로 앉으면서
Sit on the axis of your leg in front of you.

반대쪽발로 상대방을 공격하는 기술이다.
It's a technique of attacking the other side while rotating on your opposite foot.

8) 무릎차기
(Moorupchagi–Knee kicks)

무릎차기는 자신의 무릎을 접어 상대방을 공격하는 기술이다.
Knee kicks are skills to fold one's knees and attack the other.

앞서기로 자세를 잡은 후
You're standing in front of him,

한쪽 무릎을 접어서 들고 목표를 가격한다.
One knee of yours folds up and hits the target.

9) 옆차기 (Yopchagi-side kick)	옆차기는 한쪽 다리를 접었다가 펴면서 발 날로 차는 기술이다. A side kick is a technique of folding and stretching one of your legs to attack the other with a foot blade.

앞서기로 자세를 잡은 후
You're standing in front of him,

한쪽다리를 접은 후
After you've folded one of your legs,

다리를 펴면서 차는 기술이다. 이때 발 날을 만들어서 공격하도록 한다.
As you stretch your legs, a car is a skill. At this point, make a foot blade.

제6장 >>> 기초술기

(Gicho sulki-Basic techniques)

기초술기는 상대방이 본인의 손을 잡았을 경우 손을 빼는 동작부터 꺾는 동작까지 포함되어 있다.

The basic skills involve removing your hand/wrist from when an attacker grabs you by the wrist. These skills utilise techniques to release yourself from the hold and then a counter strike.

1) 잡힌 손 빼는 기술(Jabhinson ppaeneungisul-Hand removal skills from wrist grabs)

손 빼기는 상대방이 손목을 잡고 놓지 않을 경우 빼는 방법을 말한다.

Skipping refers to the method of removing a person if he or she holds the wrist and does not release it.

손빼기 1수 - Son bbaegi (hand release) technique number 1

〈상대방이 손목을 잡았을 경우 손 빼는 연습을 하기 전에 서로 예의를 갖추도록 한다.〉
〈When practicing any techniques with a partner, respect and politeness must always be shown to each other.〉

◁ 상대방과 마주보고 선 후
Stand facing each other

서로 허리를 굽혀 인사를 한 후 호신술 연습을 한다. ▷
Bow down to each other by bending at the waist before practicing the basic self-defense techniques

◁ 상대방이 오른 손목을 잡았을 경우
The attacker grabs your right wrist

오른 발과 잡힌 쪽 오른 손을
왼쪽으로 뻗으면서 손을 뺀 후 ▷
Step your right foot forward and to the left. At the same time start twisting your right-hand counter-clockwise as you push your right hand to the left along with your right foot. This will release your wrist from their grasp

◁ 팔꿈치를 구부려 접고 양 손을 모아

Continue the motion of your right arm and bring it further back to your left side as you bend your elbow and create a fist. Place your left hand on your right fist for extra support

상대의 얼굴을 공격한다. ▷

Strike the attacker' s face with your elbow.

손빼기 2수 - Son bbaegi (hand release) technique number 2

◁ 상대방이 한쪽 손을 잡았을 경우
The attacker grabs your right wrist

잡힌 손을 위로 들면서 1보 전진한 후 ▷
Step out to the right with your right foot while raising your right arm up with your palm facing outwards

◁ 시계방향으로 회전을 하면서
Step forward with your left foot and go under their arm while turning your body clockwise

1보 뒤로 빠진 후 ▷
Take one step back with your right foot and bring your arm downwards in a chopping action

◁ 잡힌 손을 회전력을 이용하여 뺀 후
Continue the vertical rotational force of your arm to remove your hand

상대의 뒷목을 내리친 후 ▷
Then strike to the back of attacker' s neck with a knife hand strike

◁ 상대방을 제압한다.
powerful strike will be able to incapaciatate the attacker.

손빼기 3수 - Son bbaegi (hand release) technique number 3

◁ 상대방이 손목을 잡아오면
The attacker grabs your right wrist

잡힌 손을 시계반대 방향으로
돌리면서
손바닥을 편다. ▷
Rotate your right arm counter-clockwise while opening your hand such that your palm ends up facing forward and your elbow is down.

◁ 오른발과 잡힌 손을
얼굴 쪽으로 뻗으면서
손을 뺀다.
At the same step forward with your right foot and strike the attacker' s face with an open palm. This motion will release your wrist from their grip and provide a counter-attack simultaneously.

손빼기 4수 – Son bbaegi (hand release) technique number 4

◁ 상대방이 손목을 잡았을 경우
The attacker grabs your right wrist

잡힌 손의 팔꿈치를 45도로 접어
손끝을 상대방의 얼굴을 향하게
한 후 1보 전진한 후 ▷
Open your hand and step in with your right foot while bending your elbow creating a 45 degree angle from the vertical

◁ 팔꿈치를 위쪽으로 밀어올린 후 손을 뺀 다음

Push your elbow straight up towards the attacker' s face. This action will release your wrist from their grasp

수도로 상대의 목덜미를 내려친다. ▷

With the hand that has been released strike the attacker' s neck with a knife hand strike.

손빼기 5수 - Son bbaegi (hand release) technique number 5

〈 상대방이 한쪽 손목을 잡았을 경우
The attacker grabs your right wrist

반대쪽 발을 뒤로 1보 뺀 후 〉
Take one step with your left foot

◁ 시계반대방향으로 회전을 하면서
Turn you body counter-clockwise as you step around with your left foot

반대손날로 상대의 뒷목을 가격한 후 ▷
Continue your rotation and strike the attacker' s neck with a knife hand strike using your other hand. As you do this rotation twist and pull your captured wrist out of their grasp

◁ 다시 반대로 회전하면서 팔꿈치로 명치를 가격한 후

Turn back the other way and using the arm that you have just released from their grasp, strike the attacker in the chest with your elbow

등주먹으로 얼굴을 가격한 후 ▷

Follow up with a back-fist strike to the face using the same arm by rotating the forearm around the elbow as a pivot point

◁ 제압한다.

Powerful and quick strikes will incapacitate the attacker.

2) 잡힌 손목 역으로 꺾는 기술(Jabhinsonmok yeogeulo kkeokkneun kisul-Joint lock skills from wrist grabs)

손목 수는 상대방이 손목을 잡았을 경우, 상대방이 잡은 손에서 빼려고 했는데 손이 빠지지 않을 경우 상대의 손목을 꺾어 제압하는 것을 말한다.

These techniques are not designed to remove the wrist directly from the attacker's grasp but rather their attack is then used against tem by applying a joint locking technique to subdue them.

손목수 1수 - Sonmoksu technique number 1

◁ 상대방이 왼손으로 오른 손목을 잡았을 경우
The attacker grabs your right wrist with their left hand

잡힌 손을 반대쪽으로 밀었다가 ▷
Step your right foot forward and pushed your right across your body to your left hand side. This motion is similar to son bbaegi technique number 1 described in the previous section

◁ 다시 본래의 위치로 이동시켜 손을 높이 든다.

Then bring your hand back to where it was originally but continue the motion so that you rotate your arm up high on your right-hand side with your palm facing out.

이때 상대방의 엄지와 검지 사이의 합곡(合谷) 혈(穴) 자리를 누르고 난 후 ▷

Use your left hand to grab their left hand. Place your thumb on the pressure point located in the webbing between the thumb and index finger (called Large Intestine 4 (LI 4)) and use your other fingers to reach around the back of their palm to secure a strong grip on their hand

◁ 왼손을 앞쪽으로 비틀어 내린 후 잡혔던 오른손을 뺀 후 상대의 팔꿈치에 대고

Rotate your body to the left and use your left hand to pull their arm to your left-hand side while extending their arm. This motion will twist their upe body and bend them forward. At this point you should keep their hand vertically flat with their little finger side at the top

체중을 이동하여 제압한다. ▷

Apply force by pressing down with your forearm onto the pressure point and elbow while lifting with your left hand. Increase the pressure downwards to drop the attacker down to the ground.

손목수 2수 - Sonmoksu technique number 2

《상대방이 손목을 잡았을 경우
The attacker grabs your right wrist

잡히지 않은 왼손을
상대의 손목에 대고》
Rotate your right arm clockwise, keeping your elbow down. Use your left hand to grab the attacker' s left hand

◁ 잡힌 손을 비틀어

Close up image. Use your fingers to reach across the back of their hand to grab the otherside of it ensuring a secure grip

상대의 손과 악수하듯 포갠 후 ▷

Remove your hand but then slide the webbing between your thumb and forefinfger between the attacker' s own fingers. This resembles a hand-shake except the attacker' s hand is upside down

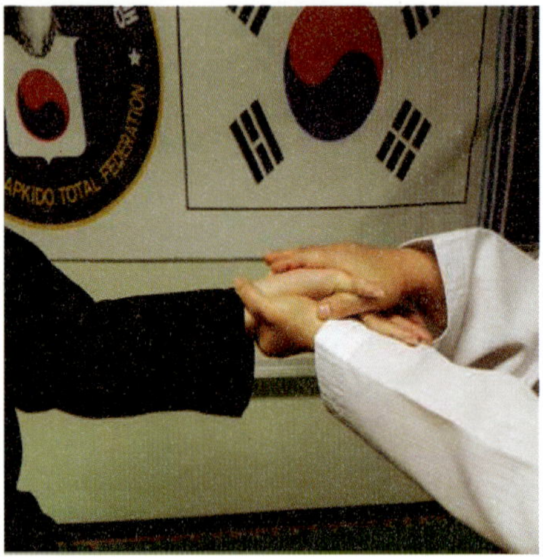

◁ 왼손을 시계방향으로 비틀면서

Twist their hand clockwise while stepping in towards them to drive their elbow in to their stomach.

아래쪽으로 누르고 ▷

Make a large circle clockwise with your arms while keeping the twisting pressure on their hand. This will twist the attacker so that their back is towards you. Press their hand down towards the ground.

◁ 상대방을 넘어트리면서 제압한다.

The attacker can be subdued by keeping the joint lock on.

손목수 3수 – Sonmoksu technique number 3

《상대방이 손목을 잡았을 경우 잡힌 손의 엄지손가락을 벌려 상대의 손목을 잡고 난 후

The attacker grabs your right wrist. Open your thumb and grab your opponent by the wrist as you push your right hand up and to the right. Your thumb needs to be on the inside of their wrist

잡히지 않은 왼손으로 상대방의 주관절 아래쪽에 있는 척택(尺澤) 혈(穴)자리를 누르고 난 후》

With your free left hand, grab their elbow and use your thumb to press on the pressure point located in the muscle on the lower-inside part of the elbow (called Heart 3 〈HT 3〉)

◁ 양손을 높이 들며 왼발을 1보 전진시킨 후
Raise both hands high, step with your left foot forward

회전하면서 들어간다. ▷
Bring your right foot through as you step under their arm and as you rotate your body clockwise.

◁ 뒷쪽에서 오른손을 뺀 후
Remove your right hand from their wrist.

상대의 팔 아래에 넣어 ▷
Slide your right arm under your attacker's arm and place your knife hand up on their shoulder

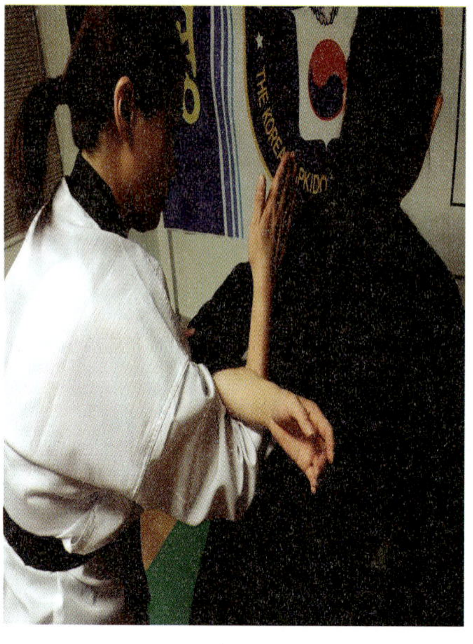

◁ 열십자(十)로 팔을 고정하여 제압한다.
Hold their arm as shown while keeping your left hand on their elbow. Apply pressure forwards and don with your right hand.

손목수 4수 - Sonmoksu technique number 4

◁ 상대방이 손목을 잡았을 경우
The attacker grabs your right wrist

잡힌 손목을 시계 반대 방향으로 돌린 후 양손으로 상대의 손목을 잡고 ▷
Rotate your hand counter-clockwise and reverse the grip by grabbing the attackers own wrist with your thumb and forefinger. The rest of your fingers should be grasping the attacker' s hand. Use your free hand to help secure the hold

〈 왼발이 오른쪽으로 1보 전진하면서
팔을 높이 든다.
Step our left foot forward as you
raise your arms.

팔 아래로 회전하여 들어간 후 〉
Step your right foot through and
rotate your body clockwise as you go
under their arm

◁ 뒤쪽에서 팔을 꺾어 잡은 후
Twist their arm and bend it up behind their back to create a hammer lock

왼손을 상대의 오른쪽 어깨에 대고 ▷
Keep your right hand on their wrist but release your left hand and put it on their right shoulder

◁ 왼발을 상대의 왼쪽 무릎 뒷쪽(안오금)을 밟은 후 제압한다.
Use your left foot to kick the back of their left knee and stomp it down to drop the attacker down to the ground by pulling their torso backwards and down. Note: you can also control the opponent on the ground by dropping them on top their arm, trapping it underneath them and putting pressure on their chest.

손목수 5수 - Sonmoksu technique number 5

◁ 상대방이 손목을 잡았을 경우

The attacker grabs your right wrist

잡힌 손을 시계 반대방향으로 돌리면서 잡고 난 후 왼손으로 손가락을 잡은 후 ▷

Rotate your hand counter-clockwise to reverse the grip. Use your free left hand to grab their left hand, placing your thumb on the pressure point LI 4 located in the webbing between the thumb and index finger

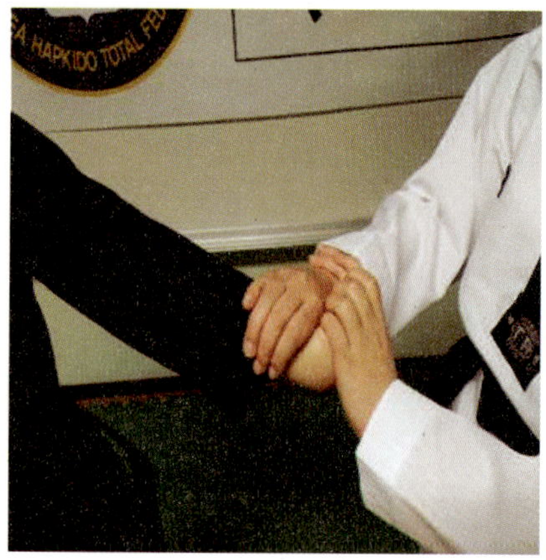

◁ 오른손은 오른쪽과 아래쪽으로 비틀고, 왼손은 왼쪽 방향과 위쪽 방향으로 비틀면서 제압한다.

Use your right hand to twist their forearm towards you, twisting downwards, while using your left hand to twist their wrist and rotate their hand updwards. This creates what is often called an S-lock.

손목수 6수 - Sonmoksu technique number 6

◁ 상대방이 손목을 잡았을 경우
The attacker grabs your right wrist.

잡힌 손을 옆으로 밀면서 1보
전진한 후 ▷
Rotate your hand to reverse the grip and capture the attacker' s hand as you stp forward and to the right with your right foot.

◁ 다른 한 손으로 상대의 반대쪽 어깨에 손을 댄 후

Place your left hand on the attacker' s right shoulder as you start to step through with your left leg

다리를 뒤쪽에 댄 후, 한손은 당기고 어깨에 댄 손은 밀면서 ▷

Use your left leg to reap their left leg by hooking behind their knee. Simultaneoulsy pulled right hand backwards and push the shoulder of the attacker to help unbalance them

◁ 상대를 밀어 넘어트린다.

Continue the push, pull and reaping actions to throw the attacker to the ground.

손목수 7수 - Sonmoksu technique number 7

◁ 상대방이 손목을 잡았을 경우
The attacker grabs your right wrist

잡힌 손을 뺀 후 다른 손으로
상대방의 손목을 바꿔 잡고 ▷
Take your hands off the hook, use the other hand to change the other person's wrist.

◁ 다른 손으로 상대의 주관절을 누른 후
Press the opponent's middle arm with the other hand

상대의 팔을 높이 들어 ▷
Raise your opponent's arm high

◁ 시계방향으로 회전을 한 후
Turn clockwise, then

넘어트려 제압한다. ▷
Continue the push, pull and reaping actions to throw the attacker to the ground.

3) 잡힌 옷을 이용한 의복술기(Jabhin oseul iyonghan uiboksulki - Joint lock skills from clothing grabs)

의복수는 상대방이 옷을 잡거나 허리띠 또는 멱살을 잡았을 경우 상대방을 제압하는 기술이다.

A technique that overpowers an opponent when he or she holds a garment or a belt or a collar.

상대방이 허리띠를 잡았을 경우 1
(Defence against being grabbed by the belt technique number 1)

◁ 상대방이 허리띠를 잡고 있을 경우
The attacker grabs you by the belt with their palm facing down

상대방의 주관절을 가격한 후 ▷
Strike the attacker' s elbow downwards with a right-hand knife hand as you step in with your right foot. This strike is to bring the attacker off balance and to bend their arm.

◁ 한 손으로 상대방의 턱을 잡고
Use your right hand to grab behind the attacker' s head and your left hand to apply pressure to their chin.

다른 한손으로는 머리를 동시에 잡으면서 ▷

Your right hand uses a pulling action and your left hand uses a pushing action to push their head backwards while twisting in a clockwise direction

◁ 옆으로 돌리면서 넘어트린다.

Continue to twist their head and take them to the ground.

상대방이 멱살을 잡아 올 경우 2
(Defence against getting grabbed by the lapel 2)

◁ 상대방이 멱살을 잡아오면
The attacker has grabbed your left lapel with their right hand

한 손으로 상대의 손목을 잡고 ▷
Use your right hand to grab their right hand, placing your thumb on the pressure point LI 4 located in the webbing between the thumb and index finger. Rotate their hand so that their hand is vertical with their little finger on top

◁ 다른 손으로 주관절 가까이 팔을 잡고 비틀면서

With your right hand keep their captured hand on your chest. Use your left hand on their forearm to twist their forearm towards you, twisting downwards, while using your right hand to twist their wrist and rotate their hand updwards. Thereby creating the S-lock

1보 전진하면서 누르고 제압한다. ▷

Press and hold as you step forward into a front bending stance apply pressure dowards and towards the attacker.

제 7 장 중급반

(Junggeubban - Intermediate techniques)

1) 주먹으로 공격해올 때 방어법 (Jumeogeulo gonggyeoghaeol ttae bangeobeob - Defences from someone punching you)

상대방이 주먹으로 공격해 올 경우 방어하는 방법을 말한다.

This refers to how to defend against an attacker who is punching you.

상대방이 주먹으로 공격해 올 경우 1
(Defence against a punch to the face technique 1)

◁ 상대방과 마주보고 서있는 상태에서

You are standing facing your attacker with each of you in a stance with the right foot back

상대방이 주먹으로 얼굴을 향해 공격해 오면 ▷

The attacker steps forward towards you with their right foot and simultaneously punches to your face with their right fist. Step backwards with your left foot and execute a right hand, knife hand block. Use your left hand to deflect the incoming punch from inside to outside with a knife hand

◁ 주먹 공격을 막은 손으로 상대방의 팔을 아래로 내린 후

Circle your left arm counter-clockwise to bring their arm down low where you can capture their wrist with both hands

반대 손으로 상대방의 손목을 잡고 ▷

Slide your left hand up to their elbow and use your thumb to apply pressure to point on the top side of the crease of the elbow (called Large Intestine 11 〈LI 11〉)

◁ 반대 손으로 상대방의 주관절을 잡은 후

Raise your arms high so that you can rotate clockwise under the attacker' s arm

시계반대 방향으로 회전을 하여 ▷
Bring your right foot through as you rotate under the attacker' s arm and create a bend in their arm

◁ 아래쪽으로 당겨 누른 후
Pull their arm down towards the ground to unbalance them

상대방을 제압한다. ▷
Continue rotating your body and pressing their arm down to force the attacker all the way to the ground. Keep pressure on their arm to subdue the attacker.

상대방이 주먹으로 하복부를 공격해올 경우 2
(Defence against a punch to the abdomen 2)

〈 상대방과 마주 본 상태에서
You are standing facing your attacker with each of you in a stance with the right foot back

상대방이 주먹으로 하복부를 공격해 올 경우 〉
The attacker steps forward towards you with their right foot and simultaneously punches to your abdomen with their right fist. Use a low cross block with knife hands, with your right hand underneath your left

◁ 양 손을 교차하여 상대의 주먹을 방어한 후

Start to rotate the attacker' s arm counter-clockwise to bring it up higher and capture their wrist with your left hand

교차된 손을 빠르게 시계반대방향으로 회전시켜 상대의 손을 바꿔 잡은 후 ▷

Continue the rotation and apply pressure with your ight hand to create a wrist lock. This lock is oten called a v-lock

〈 오른발을 축으로 왼발을 회전 시킨 후

This photos shows the reverse side of the above image so that you can see the position of the hands

상대방의 손독을 꺾어 제압한다. 〉

Bring your left foot further around behind you to continue the rotation to take the attacker down to the ground. The attacker can be subdued with various joint locks and or strikes

2) 의복 수(4수)- Uiboksu (defences against clothing grabs)

의복 수는 상대방이 옷을 잡고 공격해 올 경우 본인의 옷을 이용하여 상대를 제압하는 것을 말한다.

Defending against clothing grabs refers to the ability to use the attack of someone grabbing you by your clothing against them.

의복수 1수 - Uiboksu technique number 1

◁ 상대방이 팔소매 부분을 잡아 올 경우
The attacker has grabbed your right lower sleeve with their left hand

잡히지 않은 반대 손으로 본인의 옷과 상대의 손을 동시에 잡는다. ▷
Using your free left hand place a thumb on the sleeve near their thumb and reach your fingers across the back of their hand to get a secure grip on their hand

◁ 잡혔던 손을 상대방의 앞쪽으로 뻗으면서

Rotate their hand vertically so that their little finger is on top. At the same time rotate your right-hand counter-clockwise and place a knife-hand on top of their wrist

손이 잡혔던 쪽의 발을 앞쪽으로 1보 전진하면서 제압한다. ▷

Step forward with your right foot into a front bending stance and push your right hand down and forward while using your left hand to twist their caught hand vertically upwards.

의복수 2수 - Uiboksu technique number 2

◁ 상대방이 팔소매 중간 정도를 잡았을 경우

The attacker has grabbed your right sleeve at the elbow with their left hand

잡히지 않은 반대 손으로 상대의 중팔 아래 옷깃을 잡아 당기고 ▷

Using your free left hand grab their sleeve at the elbow and start pulling it down and to the left

《 잡혔던 부분의 손을 가로로 접어 상대의 손이 움직이지 못하게 고정 한 후

As you start pulling with your left hand, rotate your right hand counter-clockwise until it is horizontally across your chest, capturing their hand between your forearm and your chest

상대의 팔을 들어 세운 후 그 아래로 돌아 들어가서 》

Continue to rotate your right arm counter-clockwise and push your left hand to the right and upwards as you step with your left foot to go under their arm

◁ 손을 어깨 부위에 상대의 손과 열십자(十)로 고정을 한 후
Bring your right foot through then slide your right hand up between their arm and back until you reach their shoulder. You should have their arm bent back behind them in a hammer lock as shown in the picture

한발을 1보 내딛으며 제압을 한다. ▷
Take one step forward and push their shoulder forward and down.

의복수 3수 - Uiboksu technique number 3

◁ 상대방이 어깨를 잡아오면

The attacker has grabbed you by your shoulder with their left hand

잡히지 않은 반대 손으로 상대의 손을 움켜잡은 후 ▷

Use your free left hand to grab their left hand, placing your thumb on the pressure point LI 4 located in the webbing between the thumb and index finger.

◁ 시계반대방향으로 90도로 비틀면서 1보 앞으로 나가면서

Rotate their hand 90 degrees counter-clockwise so that the little finger is on top as shown in the picture. Take one step forward with your right foo

팔꿈치를 세워 상대의 주관절 부위를 압박하며 제압한다. ▷

Raise your elbow up then drop it down onto their arm with force as you drop your weight and sink lower to increase the force.

의복수 4수 - Uiboksu technique number 4

《 상대방이 멱살을 잡아 올 경우
The attacker has grabbed you by your right lapel with their left hand

반대 손으로 상대의 손을 옷과 함께 움켜잡은 후 》
Use your free left hand to grab their lefrt hand, placing your thumb on the pressure point LI 4 located in the webbing between the thumb and index finger

〈 잡은 손을 왼쪽으로 90도 비틀면서 반대 손으로 손목 바깥쪽을 잡은 후
Rotate their hand 90 degrees so that their hand is vertical with their little finger on top. Grab their wrist with your right hand. Twist their forearm towards you with your right hand, twisting downwards, while using your left hand to twist their wrist and rotate their hand upwards. Thereby creating the S-lock.

1보 앞으로 전진 하면서 제압한다. 〉
Press and hold as you step forward into a front bending stance applying pressure downwards and towards the attacker.

3) 안손목수/악수수 (3수)(Ansonmoksu/aksu-defences against cross wrist grabs/hand shakes)

안손목수는 상대방과 서로 악수를 하는 상황 또는 유사한 방법으로 손을 잡아 올 경우 상대방을 제압하기 위해 활용하는 술기의 일종이다.

These defences can be used for both having your wrist grabbed by an attacker who grabs you with the same hand (eg. their right hand grabs your right wrist - a cross grab), or for a hand shake as the principles and techniques are the same. Some people may use a hand shake under false pretences or as a trick to be able to grab you before doing a different type of attack or even just to squeeze your hand and cause pain and or intimidation.

안손목수 1수 - Ansonmoksu technique number 1

◁ 상대방과 악수하는 동작에서
You are shaking hands with another person

상대방이 손에 힘을 주거나 공격할 의사를 보일 경우 반대 손으로 중지권을 쥐고 ▷

If the other person shows their intention to attack or intimidate you use the middle knuckle of your free hand to press firmly while twisting against the middle of the back of their hand

◁ 반대 손으로 상대의 손등을 휘감아 누르면서

The pressing on the back of their hand will help loosen their grip. Then rotate your hand counter-clockwise as your grab their wrist with your left and remove your right hand from their grasp

오른발이 1보 전진하면서
비튼 후 ▷
Step forward with your right foot and apply pressure with your right hand both downwards and counter-clockwise simultaneously

◁ 밖으로 회전을 하면서 상대방을 제압한다.
Once you have taken the attacker to the ground you can control them with various joint locks and or strikes.

안손목수 2수 - Ansonmoksu technique number 2

◁ 상대방이 악수하듯 손을 잡아 올 경우

You are shaking hands with another person

잡히지 않은 반대 손으로 곡택(谷澤) 혈(穴) 자리를 누르고 난 후 ▷

Use your left thumb to apply pressure to the point on the top side of the crease of the elbow at LI 11, as you grab

their elbow.

◁ 상대의 팔을 높이 들어 세운 후
Swing both of your arms up high to the right

그 아래로 회전하여 들어간 후 ▷
Step forward with your left foot as you move under their arm

◁ 상대의 손목을 접혀있는 상태로 잡은 후
As you turn your body clockwise bend their arm at the elbow

아래쪽으로 누르면서 ▷
Push their arm forward and down

◁ 상대의 중심을 뒤쪽으로 밀어 넘어뜨린 후

Continue pushing forward and down to take the attacker down to the floor

손목이 지면에 닿게 한 후 눌러 제압한다. ▷

Put their wrist on the ground underneath their arm and press their elbow down to the ground to hold them in position.

안손목수 3수 - Ansonmoksu technique number 3

◁ 상대방이 악수하듯 손을 잡아오면
The attacker grabs your right wrist with their right hand in a cross grab

반대 손으로 상대의 주관절에 손을 뻗어 상대의 손이 펴지게 한 후 ▷
Rotate your hand counter-clockwise and reverse the grip so that you are holding them by the wrist. Step your left foot forward as you raise their arm up to your right side and raise your left arm so that it crosses under their elbow

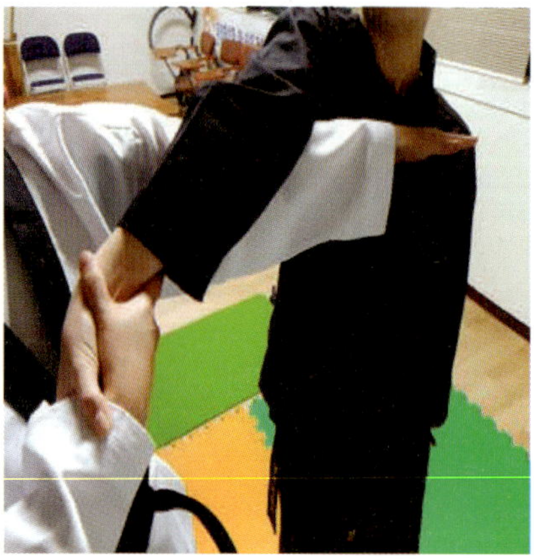

◁ 손끝은 상대의 반대쪽 쇄골 부위에 고정을 한 후
Place your fingertips on top of their clavicle as shown or alternatively on top their shoulder if you can reach. Apply pressure down on their right wrist with your right hand and raise your left arm to create an arm-bar

다시 두 손으로 손목을 잡은 후 ▷

Release your left hand and slide it down to grab their wrist to get a secure grip

◁ 상대의 팔을 어깨에 대고 들면서 제압한다.

Bring your right foot back into a horse-riding stance with your back to the attacker and put their elbow on top of your shoulder as you pull down on the arm with both hands. This technique can break the attacker' s arm if you pull down with strength. To create the arm-bar effectively the attacker' s hand should be palm up which will have their elbow downwards.

제8장 고급반

(Gogeubban - Advanced techniques)

1) 방권술/주먹막기 (3수)(Bangkwonsul/jumeokmakki-punch defence/ fist blocking)

방권술은 상대방이 주먹으로 공격해 올 경우 상대의 주먹을 막고 제압하는 호신 기법을 말한다.

Bangkwonsul or punch defence refers to the self-defense techniques that are used against a punch attack and in which the defender then subdues the attacker.

방권술 1수 - Bangkwonsul technique number 1

◁ 상대방과 마주 본 상태에서
You are standing facing your attacker with each of you in a stance with the right foot back

상대방이 주먹을 지르면 ▷
The attacker punches to your face with their right fist while stepping forward
with their right foot. Use your left-hand to create a circular block from the outside to the inside.

◁ 왼손으로 상대의 팔을 막으면서
Use your left hand to block the incoming punch from the inside

◁ 상대방의 손목을 잡은 후
Grab the attacker’ s wrist with your left hand as you step forward with your right foot

반대 손으로 상대의 어깨를 밀면서 ▷
Then step your right foot behind the attacker’ s front leg and push the attacker’ s left shoulder with your right hand

《 바깥쪽으로 회전을 하면서 다리를 걸고

Use your right leg to reap their front leg while pushing their shoulder with your right hand and pulling with your left hand to off-balance the attacker

밀어 넘어트린다. 》

Continue the motion to take the attacker to the ground.

방권술 2수 - Bangkwonsul technique number 2

◁ 상대방과 마주보고 서있는 자세에서

You are standing facing your attacker with the attacker in a stance with their right foot back, while you are in a stance with your left foot back

상대방이 주먹으로 공격해오면 한손으로 손을 막고 ▷

The attacker punches to your face with their right fist while stepping forward with their right foot. Use a right-hand knife-hand to create a circular block from the outside to the inside

◁ 다른 손으로 상대의 팔 가운데(주관절)에 반대 손을 대면서

Continue the circular rotation and grab the attacker' s wrist with your right hand as you move your free left hand up towards their elbow

반대 발을 1보 전진시키며 수도를 댄 후 ▷

Rotate their wrist and apply your forearm to pressure point TW 11 just above the elbow and press down as you step forward with your left foot to create an arm-bar

〈 전환법을 계속 진행하면서

Rotate your body clockwise as you step your right around behind you

상대의 중심을 무너뜨린 후 제압한다. 〉

Continue the rotation and force downwards as you take the attacker down to the ground in a spiral motion. You can apply various joint locks and or strikes to subdue the attacker on the ground.

방권술 3수 - Bangkwonsul technique number 3

◁ 상대방과 마주보고 서있는 자세에서
You are standing facing your attacker with the attacker in a stance with their right foot back, while you are in a stance with your left foot back

상대방이 주먹으로 공격해 오면 ▷
The attacker punches to your face with their right fist while stepping forward with their right foot. Use your left-hand to create a circular block from the outside to the inside

◁ 안쪽으로 돌리면서 손을 막고

Continue the circular rotation

시계방향으로 돌리면서 ▷

Bringing the attacker' s arm down in a clockwise motion

◁ 다시 어깨선까지 돌려 막은 후

Circle your arm back up to shoulder level

상대의 손을 어깨에 걸쳐 고정한 후 ▷
Bend your elbow to capture their arm against your neck/shoulder in an arm-bar while pulling your arm in tight against your chest to apply pressure to their elbow joint

◁ 반대 손으로 상대의 목을 눌러 제압한다.
Step your right foot around in a clockwise direction while pressing down on the attacker' s neck and pulling their arm in tight to bring them down to the ground. By bringing them forward on to their stomach you can continue the arm-bar pressure to subdue the attacker.

2) 방족술 (3수)(Bangjoksul-kick defence)

방족술은 상대방이 발로 공격해 올 경우 상대의 발을 이용해 제압하는 것을 말한다.

Bangjoksul or kick defence refers to the self-defense techniques that are used against a kicking attack and in which the defender then subdues the attacker.

방족술 1수 - Bangjoksul technique number 1

◁ 상대방과 마주 보고 서있는 상태에서

You are standing facing your attacker with each of you in a stance with the right foot back

상대방이 발등으로 공격해 올 경우 상대의 다리를 한 팔로 들어 안고 ▷
The attacker kicks at your torso with a rear foot roundhouse kick. Use your left arm to hook under the kicking leg to capture it

◁ 다른 한손으로 상대의 어깨에 손을 대고 밀면서
Step forward with your right foot and place your right hand on their left shoulder

상대의 다리를 걸어 ▷
Hook your right leg behind the attacker' s grounded leg

◁ 회전을 하면서 상대방을 밀어 넘어트려 제압을 한다.
Push the attacker' s shoulder and pull their leg as you rotate your torso and trip them over your own leg to take the attacker down to the ground.

방족술 2수 - Bangjoksul technique number 2

◁ 상대방과 마주보고 선 상태에서

You are standing facing your attacker with the attacker in a stance with their right foot back, while you are in a stance with your left foot back

상대방이 옆차기로 공격해 올 경우 ▷

The attacker kicks at your torso with a rear foot side kick. Hook under their foot at their ankle to keep their leg in the air with your left hand

〈 왼발이 전진하면서 전환을 한 후 한손으로 다리를 막으며 잡고 나서

Step your left foot forward and turn your body clockwise while bringing your right foot around and maintaining the hold on their foot

다른 발로 상대방의 안오금을 하단 옆차기로 찬다. 〉

Kick the back of the attacker's knee with your right foot in a side kick position across their knee

〈 상대방이 넘어지면 돌아서서 제압한다.

Keep pressing their knee down with your foot to force the attacker forward and on to the ground.

방족술 3수 - Bangjoksul technique number 3

◁ 상대방과 마주보고 선 상태에서
You are standing facing your attacker with each of you in a stance with the right foot back

상대방이 뒤 돌려차기(회축)로 공격해 오면 ▷
The attacker kicks at your torso with a rear foot turning back kick

《 오른발을 접어서 들고 기다린 후
Bring your right foot through raising it

상대방의 둔부(엉덩이)와 다리 연결부위를 발바닥으로 대면서 》
Place the sole of your foot on the hip area of the leg that is kicking you

◁ 상대를 밀어버린다.
Push kick the attacker to unbalance and force the attacker to the ground.

상대가 일어나기 전에 제압을 한다. ▷
Be ready and hold your position in case the attacker tries to get up.

3) 양손목수(전) 3수 및 (후) 1수(Yangsonmoksu-double wrist grab 〈front and back〉)

양손목수는 상대방이 앞에서 양쪽 손목을 잡았을 경우, 상대방을 제압하기 위해 힘 이용법을 활용하여 제압하는 기술을 말한다.

Yangsonmoksu or double wrist grab refers to self-defence techniques in which an attacker grabs hold of both of your wrists with both of their hands. These techniques are used to control and subdue the attacker.

양손목수(전) 1수 - Yangsonmoksu front technique number 1

◁ 상대방이 양 손목을 잡았을 경우
The attacker holds both of your wrists from the front

두 손바닥을 똑같이 모은 후
1보 앞으로 나가면서 상대방을 주시한 후▷

Place your palms together then take a step forward. Keep your eyes on the attacker

◁모은 손끝을 위로 올리면서 손을 뺀다.

Push your hands towards the face of the attacker and then up to remove them.

양손목수(전) 2수 - Yangsonmoksu front technique number 2

◁ 상대방이 양 손목을 잡았을 경우

The attacker holds both of your wrists from the front

양 손바닥을 붙인 후 위로 들어 올리면서 ▷

Place both palms together as you did in technique number 1. Then lift both of your arms up and to th right

◁ 왼발을 1보 전진시켜

Move your left foot one step forward as you rotate underneath their arms in a clockwise direction

뒤쪽으로 돌아 들어간 후 ▷

Bring your right foot back as you swing your arms downwards

◁ 양 손을 빠르게 당기면서
Complete the swing through with your arms ensuring that you do the motion quickly

손을 위로 들어 올린 후 ▷
Then raise your arms

◁ 상대의 목을 치면서 제압한다.
Use a knife hand attack to strike the attacker' s neck.

양손목수(전) 3수 - Yangsonmoksu front technique number 3

《 상대방이 양 손목을 잡았을 경우
The attacker holds both of your wrists from the front

한 손은 상팔 아래로 대고, 다른 손은 손바닥이 위쪽으로 향하게 한 후 》
Step your right foot forward as you raise your left hand and swing up your right arm placing your foearm underneath their elbow. Your aim is to create an arm-bar to unbalance the attacker

〈 다시 위쪽 팔에 댔던 손을 손목으로 이동시키고, 다른 손은 주관절 부분에 댄 후

Step your left foot around as you bring your right hand down to grab the attackers right wrist while removing your left hand from their grasp and reapply the arm-bar this time with your left arm under their right elbow

왼발을 1보 전진시켜 전환을 한 후 〉

Continue moving your left foot around

〈 팔꿈치에 대고 왼팔에 힘을 준 후 오른 손목을 당겨 강하게 압박을 한 후

Pull downwards with your right hand and raise your left arm to increase the arm-bar pressure. By applying considerable force you will unbalance the attacker bringing them up on their toes to relieve the pressure

다시 왼손이 손목 쪽으로 이동을 하고 오른팔이 상대의 겨드랑이로 이동시켜 〉

Bring your left hand back down to grab the attacker' s left wrist as you step back inwards and move your right arm underneath theirs

〈 엎어치기 자세로 한 팔을 당긴 후

Continue the rotational step back in to the attacker while bvending your knees to bring your hips lower than theirs. As you do so bring their arm over your shoulder while grabbing their upper arm with your right arm and maintaining your hold on their wrist with your left hand. (Note: this is the shoulder throw position and the shoulder throw can be completed from here, if the shoulder throw fails continue to the next step)

굽혔던 무릎을 편 후
한 팔을 감았던 손을 빼어 상대의
턱에 대고 〉

If for whatever reason the shoulder throw fails or if you chose not to continue with the motion you cn continue with the following steps. Release your right hand and bring back in to your body as you straighten your legs and rotate your torso clockwise to face the attacker partially. Elbow the attacker' s chin/jawline

◁ 밀어 넘어뜨려 제압한다.
Strike hard with your elbow to knock out the attacker.

양손목수(후) 1수는 상대방이 뒤쪽에서 양 손목을 잡았을 경우 회전을 하여 상대를 제압하는 것을 말한다.

Yangsonmoksu bbaek or rear double wrist grab refers to self-defence techniques in which an attacker grabs hold of both of your wrists with both of their hands from behind you. These techniques are used to control and subdue the attacker.

양손목수(후) 1수 - Yangsonmoksu rear technique number 1

◁ 상대방이 뒤쪽에서 양 손목을 잡았을 경우

The attacker holds both of your wrists from the rear

좌 또는 우로 몸을 돌려 ▷

Turn left then right

〈 약한 쪽을 선택한 후
Using the repeated turns select which side is the attacker' s weak side

바깥쪽으로 회전을 하여 〉
Use a twisting motion with your hand to release from one grip and turning towards the other side. In this instance you have released your left hand and rotated clockwise

《상대방의 손에서 이탈 시킨 후

Grab the attacker' s right wrist with your free left hand as your twist your right hand out of their grasp while stepping around with your left leg in the same clockwise motion

다시 상대방의 손목을 바꿔 잡은 후》

Bring the attacker' s arm across your body to create pressure on their elbow as you step your right leg back around. Then start to bring their arm back out from your body again

◁ 안쪽으로 전환을 하면서 자세를 바꾼 후

As you bring their arm out change which hand is holding the attacker' s wrist. It should now be the left hand

다시 반대쪽으로 회전을 하여 ▷

Step your right foot back the way it originally came from. As you bring their arm around in front of you their arm should be bent in the v-lock position

◁ 다리를 깊게 걸어

Step your right foot through and behind the attacker' s right leg as you apply wrist lock pressure with your free hand

상대의 중심을 무너뜨린 후 ▷

Rotate your torso as you apply rotataional and downwards pressure on the wrist lock to unbalance the attacker

◁ 넘어트려 제압한다.

Continue the motion to take the attacker to the ground. Various locks and or strikes can be applied to subdue the attacker from this position.

제9장 응용술기

(Eungyongsulki-application techniques)

응용술기는 특수기술로 단검 막기와 권총방어로 구분하였다.

Application techniques refer to a series of skills used to defend against an armed attacker. The ones presented here address being attacked by a knife (단검 - dangeom), or gun (권총 - gwonchong).

1) 단검 막기 (3수)(Dangeom makki-three techniques to defend against a knife attack)

단검 막기는 상대방이 칼로 공격해 올 경우 자신을 안전하도록 검을 막고 상대방을 제압하는 것을 말한다.

Knife blocking refers to defending against a knife attack and subduing the attacker.

단검 막기 1수 - Dangeom makki (knife blocking and defence technique number 1)

◁상대방이 칼을 들고 찌르려고 할 경우
An attacker has drawn a knife and is intent on stabbing you

상대방이 칼로 복부를 공격해 올 경우 한발을 뒤로 빼면서 양손을 교차시켜 위에서 아래로 상대의 칼 든 손을 내려 막으며 (이때 왼손이 위로 오도록 한다)▷
As the attacker stabs at your abdomen with a knife held in their right hand while stepping forward, step your right foot back to make sure you create space between the knife and your body. Use a cross hands, knife-hand block with your right hand below your left hand to press the attacking arm downwards

《 교차했던 손으로 시계반대 방향으로 손을 돌려 올리면서

Rotate your right hand counter-clockwise and adjust your left hand to grab their wrist as their hand becomes vertical

오른발-왼발 순으로 전환을 하면서 회전 가속도를 높이고 오른발로 상대의 다리 뒤쪽에 걸어 》

Step your right foot forward and through while accelerating your upper body rotation in the same counter-clockwise motion. At this point you should have created a v-lock on their attacking wrist/arm

◁ 상대방이 넘어지도록 손목을 계속 비틀면서 칼을 뺏는다.
Keep twisting the wrist so that the other person falls and take the knife

상대방이 칼을 놓았다 하더라도 무릎으로 상대의 팔을 압박하여 제압하도록 한다. ▷
Even if the attacker releases the knife, press their arm down and use your knee on their elbow to pin their arm to the ground or to break their arm if you cannot get them to release the knife.

단검 막기 2수 - Dangeom makki (knife blocking and defence technique number 2)

◁ 상대방이 칼을 들고 찌르려고 할 때
An attacker has drawn a knife and is intent on stabbing you

상대방이 칼로 복부를 공격해 올 경우 이번에는 왼쪽발이 뒤로 1보 빠지면서 양손을 교차하여 아래로 막는다(이때 오른손은 위로 가도록 한다) ▷
As the attacker stabs at your abdomen with a knife held in their right hand while stepping forward, step your left foot back to make sure you create space between the knife and your body. Use a cross hands, knife-hand block with your left hand below your right hand (opposite to technique number 1) to press the attacking arm downwards

◁ 교차하여 막은 손은 시계방향으로 돌려 상대의 손목을 꺾은 후

Rotate your left hand clockwise and adjust your right hand to grab their wrist as their hand becomes vertical. Apply a wrist lock by bending their wrist back towards their elbow, keeping their arm straight

오른발로 상대의 복부를 1차 가격한 후 ▷

Kick the attacker in the chest with your right foot

◁ 다시 왼쪽 무릎으로 상대의 어깨 관절을 눌러
Step your right foot down after the kick and use your left knee to apply pressure to the attacker' s shoulder

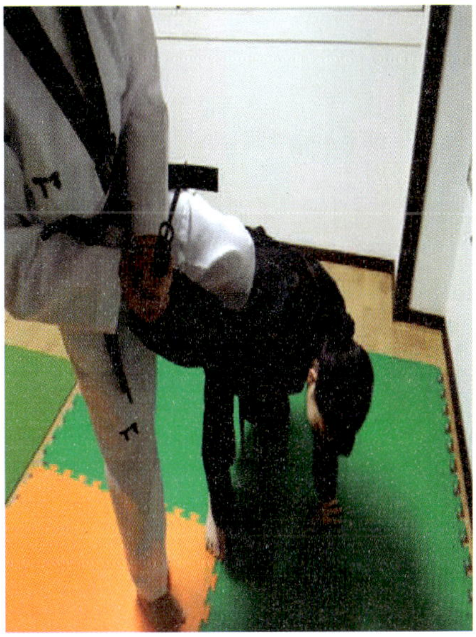

상대의 중심을 아래로 내리면서 상대방의 칼을 빼앗은 후 ▷
Use your weight on the knee to bring the attacker down

◁ 무릎으로 완전히 상대의 몸이 지면에 닿도록 한 후

Continue to force them completely to the ground

제압하도록 한다. ▷

Keep your knee and weight on their shoulder and maintain a strong grip on their wrist. Continue to apply force on the wrist lock until they drop the knife.

단검 막기 3수 - Dangeom makki (knife blocking and defence technique number 3)

◁ 상대방이 검을 거꾸로 잡고 공격해 올 경우

An attacker has drawn a knife and is intent on stabbing you in a downwards angle with a reverse grip

상대방이 칼을 거꾸로 잡고 위쪽에서 어깨 쪽으로 공격하려고 할 때 머리를 한쪽으로 비켜 피한 후 ▷

When the attacker steps their right foot forward and stabs downward with the knife in their right hand, step back with your left leg to get your body out of the way of the knife

〈 반대쪽에서 다시 거꾸로 검으로 공격해 올 때

The attacker then conducts a follow up horizontal stab from the inside to outside

상대방의 칼 잡은 손을 막은 후 손목을 잡고 〉

Intercept their right arm at the wrist with a right hand knife-hand block

〈 반대 손으로 상대의 주관절(중팔)에 대고
Capture their wrist with your right hand as you step forward with your left foot and use your left hand to apply an arm-bar at pressure point TW 11 just above the elbow

바깥으로 회전을 한 후 〉
Step your right foot around and turn your body clockwise bringing their arm down in front of your danjeon

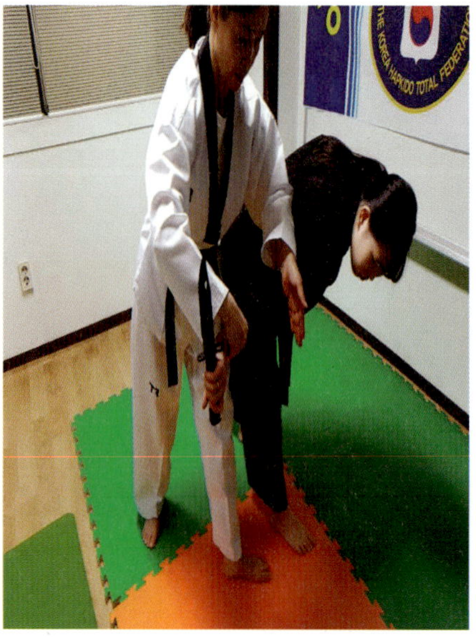

〈 체중을 이용하여 상대의 몸을 아래로 누른 후

Use your weight to press down on the arm-bar

다시 반대로 회전을 하면서 주관절을 당기면서 칼 잡은 손을 반대로 꺾으면서 〉

Step your right foot back counter-clockwise and follow with your left leg. As you rotate back bring their arm up and around while using your left hand to press on the inside of the attacker' s elbow to start bending their arm

◁ 바깥쪽으로 회전을 한 후

Place your right foot behind the attacker' s right leg as you continue to bend and twist the attacker' s arm. You can create what is called a figure-4 lock at this stage

상대방의 다리를 걸어 ▷

Take the attacker down to the ground

◁ 넘어트린 후 제압한다.
(이 때 칼은 반드시 상대방에게서 이탈되도록 한다)

Apply a joint lock such as the figure-4 lock and or strike them, then strip the knife out of their hands.

2) 권총 방어법 (2수)(Gwonchong bangeobeop-two techniques to defend against a gun being pointed at you)

상대방이 권총으로 겨눌 경우 권총을 막고 상대방을 제압하는 것을 말한다.

Gwonchong bangeobeop refers to a group of techniques used to defend oneself when an attacker points a gun at you. These technques are then used to subdue the attacker.

권총방어법 1수 - Gwonchong bangeobeop (gun defense technique number 1)

《 상대방이 권총으로 정면을 겨눌 경우

You and the attacker are facing each other. The attacker has drawn a pistol and has pointed it at your head with their right hand. Raise your hands in a non-threatening manner

왼발이 1보 전진하면서
한손은 권총 든 상대의 손목을 옆으로
밀어낸 후 ▷
Step your left foot forward and simultaneously use your left hand to quickly push the gun towards the right to make sure you ae out of the line of fire

◁ 상대의 손목을 꺾은 후
Capture the attacker' s wrist

◁ 안쪽으로 회전하면서
Grab the barrel of the gun with your right hand and push it upwards as you step your right foot forward to add force to the movement

상대방의 권총을 뺏은 후 ▷
Keep on pushing it up to remove it out of the attackers' grasp

◁ 권총 손잡이 넓은 면으로 상대의
관자놀이를 친 후
Strike the attacker' s head (temple)
with the handle of a pistol

상대방을 제압하여 마무리 한다. ▷
Take the attacker to the ground

권총방어법 2수 - Gwonchong bangeobeop (gun defense technique number 2)

◁ 상대방이 뒤쪽에서 권총으로 겨눌 경우

The attacker has approached you from behind and has pointed a pistol at the back of your head with their right hand. Raise your hands in a non-threatening manner

빠르게 우측으로 머리를 돌린 후 ▷

Quickly turn your head to the right.

〈 손으로 권총 입구를 다른 방향으로 쳐내며

Use your right hand to strike at the wrist of their hand to take the pistol off of the line of your head

바깥으로 회전을 하면서 권총 든 손목을 잡고 〉

Bring your left leg around as you capture their wrist with your right hand

◁ 빠른 회전을 하면서 반대 손으로 상대의 주관절을 눌러

Continue turning and use your left hand to apply an arm-bar at pressure point TW 11 just above the elbow

체중을 실어 아래로 누르면서 ▷

Bring their arm down in front of your danjeon as you increase the pressure to their elbow joint

◁ 다시 반대방향으로 회전을 한 후
Rotate back in the opposite direction
to bend their arm and bring it up

상대방의 몸에 붙어서 ▷
Step through with your right foot and
create a v-lock

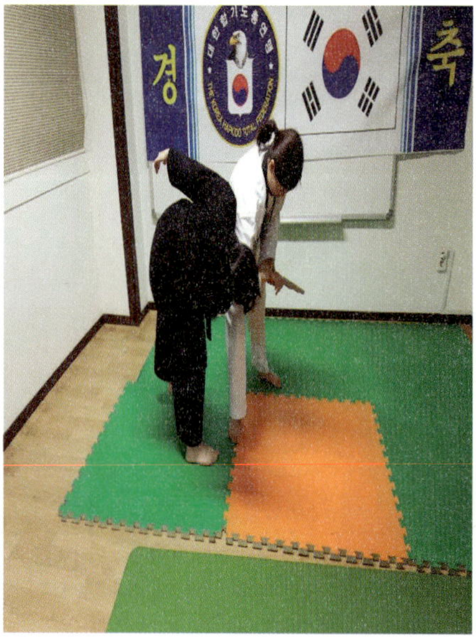

◁ 손목을 비틀어 돌리면서

Continue the rotation as well as the twisting and downward force on the wrist

상대방의 다리를 걸어 ▷

Trip the attacker using your leg

◁ 뒤쪽으로 넘어뜨리면서
Take the attacker to the ground

제압한다. ▷
Subdue the attacker using a lock or strike.

◁ 이때 상대방에게서 권총을 이탈시켜 마무리 한다.
Remove the pistol from the attacker.

제10장 >>> 용어정리

(Yong a jungri-Terminology theorem)

1) 단전호흡 : 배꼽아래 3촌 지점에 있는 "기해" 혈자리에 힘을 주고 코로 들이마시고 내뱉기

Danjeon breathing method: located just below the navel at the meridian Gihae, the danjeon is able to provide strength and energy when used for breathing through the nose.

2) 전환법 : 상대방의 힘을 이용하기 위하여 몸을 회전시키는 방법

Stepping method: allows the practitioner to use body rotation to take advantage of an attacker's power.

3) 4방전환법 : 네 방향으로 회전하는 방법

Four-way stepping method: rotation in four directions.

4) 손빼기 : 상대방이 손을 잡았을 때 손을 빼는 방법

Hands release: how to remove a your hand when an attacker grabs hold of your hand or wrist.

5) 손목수 : 상대방이 손목을 잡았을 경우 손목을 꺾는 방법

Wrist grab joint lock techniques: how to remove your hand from an attacker's grab and apply various joint locking techniques to subdue the attacker.

6) 의복수 : 상대방이 옷을 잡았을 경우 제압하는 방법

Clothing grab defences: techniques for defending yourself when you have been grabbed by your clothes.

7) 안손목수 : 악수하는 식으로 손을 잡았을 경우 꺾는 법

Inside wrist grab joint lock techniques: how to remove your hand from an attacker's grab including a handshake, and apply various joint locking techniques to subdue the attacker.

8) 방권술 : 상대방이 주먹으로 공격해 올 때 막는 법

Punch defence: how to defend against an attack from a person punching you with their fist.

9) 방족술 : 상대방이 발로 공격해 올 경우 방어법

Kick defence: how to defend against an attack from a person who is kicking you.

10) 양손목수(전) : 상대방이 앞에서 양 손목을 잡았을 경우 제압 법

Double wrist joint lock techniques (front): how to remove your hand(s) from an attacker who has grabbed both of your wrists from the front and apply various joint locking techniques to subdue the attacker.

11) 양손목수(후) : 상대방이 뒤에서 양 손목을 잡았을 경우 제압 법

Double wrist joint lock techniques (behind): how to remove your hand(s) from an attacker who has grabbed both of your wrists from behind and apply various joint locking techniques to subdue the attacker.

12) 응용술기(Application techniques) - does not match the contents should be knife and gun

(1) 단검 막기 - 단검 막기는 상대방이 칼로 공격해 올 경우 막는 방법을 말한다.

Dangeom makki (knife blocking and defence technique)-This refers to how to prevent an opponent from attacking with a knife.

(2) 권총 방어 법 - 권총 방어 법은 상대방이 권총으로 겨눌 경우 권총을 빼앗고 이를 제압하는 방법을 말한다.

Gwonchong bangeobeop(gun defense technique number 1)-This refers to how to take away a pistol and overpower it if the opponent is confronted with a pistol.

에필로그

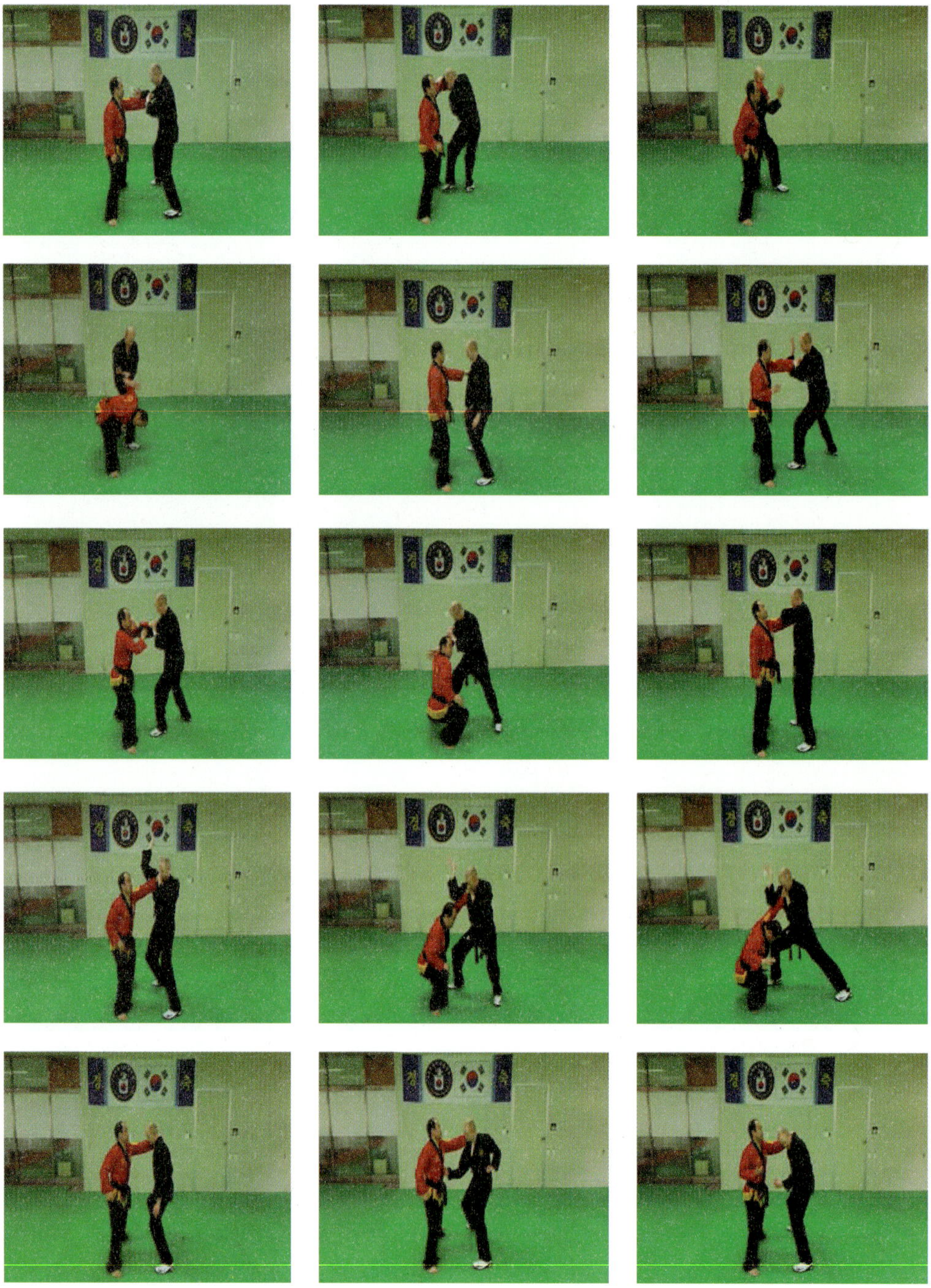

저자약력

이기세 Lee, Gi-se	순천향대학교 일반대학원 경찰학 박사 국립인천대학교 일반대학원 체육학 박사 고려대학교 교육대학원 교육학석사 전, 경찰종합학교 외래교수 전, 중국요녕중의대학 객좌교수 전, 인천시 공무원연수원 외래교수 전, 경찰교육원 외래교수 전, 우석대학교 교수 현, 경찰학회 이사 현, 범죄학회 이사 현, 국제대학교 교수
DAMIAN ADAMS (데미안 아담스)	플린더스대학교 생명공학졸업 남호주대학교 의학자 현, 호주 미래산업 연구소 재생의학 과학자 현, 호주 해태 무술관 관장 현, 한국 합기도 총연맹 호주 회장 현, 태권도 5단(국기원) 현, 합기도 4단(한국합기도 총연맹)
노성환 No, Sung-hwan	전, 인천지방경찰청 체포술 무도사범 전, 용인대학교 동양무예학과 입학심사 외래교수 전, 인천광역시 태권도 협회 심사분과위원 전, 인천광역시 태권도 협회 경기분과위원 현, 대한용무도협회 인천시대표 총감독 현, 동이무예(6개지관) 종합체육관 총관장
최영진 Choi, Young-jin	고려대학교 일반대학원 체육학 박사 수료 공주대학교 일반대학원 체육학 석사 현, 고려대학교 외래교수 현, 우석대학교 외래교수 현, 한국 사회안전 융합건강학회 간사
천인순 Cheon, In-soon	인천대학교 사회복지학 석사 남서울대학교 체육학 석사 전, 국제대학교 외래교수 현, 한국 사회안전 융합건강학회 사무국장 현, 인천대학교 평생교육원 외래교수 현, 바른자세헬스케어 활정술 아카데미 원장 현, 융합건강연구소 소장
김현동 Kim, Hyun-Dong	순천향대학교 경찰학 박사 동국대학교 경찰학 석사 현, 사단법인 한국경찰학회 이사 현, 사단법인 한국공안행정학회 이사 현, 사단법인 피해자포럼 총무위원 현, 한국민간경비학회 이사 현, 한국영상대학교 경찰행정과 교수(학과장)